T0386049

Arabian horses

by **Kate Riddle**

ALWAYS LEARNING

PEARSON

Contents

Arabian horses are one of the oldest **breeds** of horses in the world. A long time ago, they lived in the desert and were looked after by the Bedouin people. The Bedouin people live in the desert and move from place to place.

Arabian horses are strong, fast and **brave**. They were very important to the Bedouin people. The horses were used to fight in wars. They were also used for travelling long **distances** through the desert.

This is an Arabian horse in England.

Arabian horses lived closely with the Bedouin people and even today are known for working well with people. They have a kind and sweet **personality** and are also very clever. Over the years, Arabian horses became very **popular** and today they can be found all over the world.

Arabian horse facts!

Horses are measured in 'hands'. Arabian horses are between 14.1 and 15.1 hands – this is about 1.5 metres. Arabian horses are shorter than many other breeds of horses.

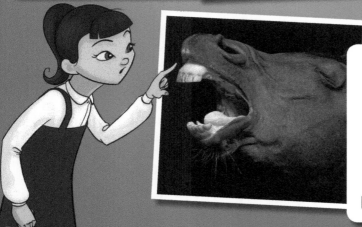

If Arabian horses are well looked after, they live for about 25–30 years. You can tell a horse's age by looking at its teeth!

Arabian horses, like other horses, can sleep standing up!

Arabian horses weigh between 360 and 500 kilograms.

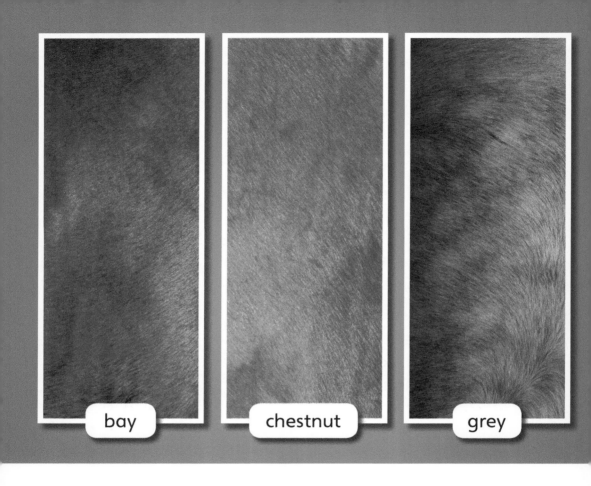

bay

chestnut

grey

There are many different colours of Arabian horses.

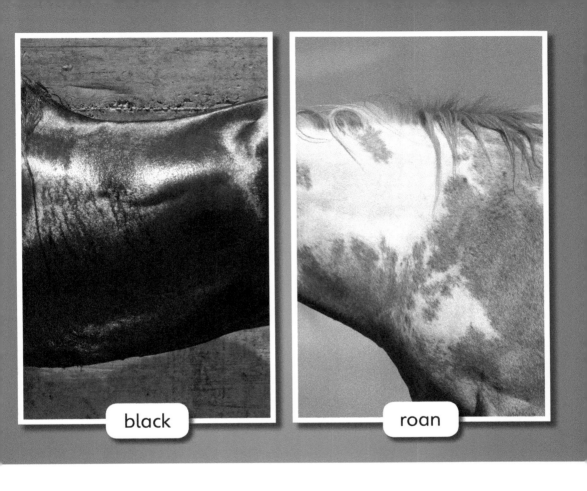

black

roan

What colours can you see?

long ears

large eyes

big nostrils

deep chest

10

long neck

Arabian horses are beautiful and have some special **features**.

short back

high tail

Arabian horses have large nostrils, a deep chest and
strong legs. This makes them good at racing.

The races can be as long as 161 kilometres!

Horses need a special passport to take part! This passport has a record of their age and their health.

Some Arabian horses are **trained** to take part in longer races. These races take place in the UAE, Qatar and Bahrain.

Arabian horses are also popular pets because they have a sweet nature. They need to be well looked after with somewhere nice to live and plenty of food and water.

It is also very important for them to
have large open spaces to exercise.

Arabian horses are still as important and loved today
as they were in the past by the Bedouin people!